FE

■ SCHOLASTIC
News
Nonfiction Readers

A Spiderling Grows Up

Pam Zollman

Children's Press®
A Division of Scholastic Inc.
New York Toronto London Auckland Sydney
Mexico City New Delhi Hong Kong
Danbury, Connecticut

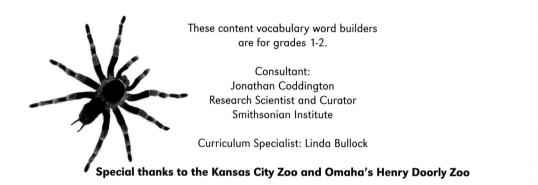

These content vocabulary word builders
are for grades 1-2.

Consultant:
Jonathan Coddington
Research Scientist and Curator
Smithsonian Institute

Curriculum Specialist: Linda Bullock

Special thanks to the Kansas City Zoo and Omaha's Henry Doorly Zoo

Photo Credits:

Photographs © 2005: Animals Animals: cover center inset, 16, 17, 21 top right (Peter Gould/OSF), 20 top left (Ralph Reinhold); Dembinsky Photo Assoc./Gary Meszaros: 15; Dwight R. Kuhn Photography: cover background, cover left inset, cover right inset, 1, 4, 5, 6, 7, 9, 10, 18, 19, 20 bottom left, 20 top right, 21 bottom, 21 top left, 23 top left, 23 bottom right; Nature Picture Library Ltd.: back cover (Jose Luis Gomez de Franciso), 11 (Duncan McEwan); Peter Arnold Inc./Hans Pfletschinger: 13; Photo Researchers, NY: 23 top right (Dante Fenolio), 2 (Barbara Strnadova); Seapics.com/Tim Rock: 23 bottom left.

Book Design: Simonsays Design!

Library of Congress Cataloging-in-Publication Data

Zollman, Pam.
  A spiderling grows up / by Pam Zollman.
    p. cm. — (Scholastic news nonfiction readers)
  Includes bibliographical references and index.
  ISBN 0-516-24946-0 (lib. bdg.)
  1. Spiders—Development—Juvenile literature. I. Title. II. Series.
  QL458.4.Z65 2005
  595.4'4139—dc22
                        2005003293

1 2 3 4 5 6 7 8 9 10 R 14 13 12 11 10 09 08 07 06 05

CONTENTS

WORD HUNT

Look for these words as you read. They will be in **bold**.

adult
(**ah**-duhlt)

moult
(mohlt)

sac
(sak)

arachnid
(uh-**rak**-nid)

eggs
(egs)

silk
(silk)

spiderling
(**spy**-dur-ling)

5

Spiderlings!

What are **spiderlings**?

Spiderlings are baby spiders.

Spiders are **arachnids**.

Arachnids have eight legs.

arachnid

These are spiderlings.

Spiderlings come from **eggs**.

A mother spider lays the eggs.

Then it wraps the eggs in a **sac**.

The sac keeps the eggs safe.

This mother spider is wrapping its eggs in a sac.

Some spiders hide their egg sacs.

Spiders use leaves to hide the sacs.

Some spiders sit with their sacs.

Some spiders carry their sacs.

egg sac

This spider is sitting with its egg sac. The sac is hidden under a leaf.

The eggs hatch inside the sac.

The spiderlings **moult**, or shed their skin, before they come out of the sac.

Then they use their fangs to cut open the sac.

Fangs are special teeth.

Look! Spiderlings are coming out of the sac.

Some spiderlings live on their own.

Some ride on their mother's back.

Some mother spiders die when the eggs hatch.

Some spiderlings eat their mother's body after it dies.

Yuck!

These spiderlings are riding on their mother's back.

All spiderlings spin **silk**.

Some make silk bridges.

Some glide away on
silk strands.

Where are these
spiderlings going?

They are going to make
new homes.

silk

These spiderlings are gliding away on silk strands.

The spiderlings moult a few more times.

That means they shed their skin again.

Now they are **adult** spiders.

a spider moulting

This spider is
all grown-up!

19

A SPIDERLING GROWS UP!

1 . . .

In the fall, a
female garden
spider lays eggs.
It makes a silk sac
to protect the eggs.

2 . . .

The eggs grow in the sac.
The spider hides the sac
under a leaf to keep it safe.

5 Look! This spider is an adult. It can spin webs that are 2 feet long!

4 The spiderlings spin silk. Some glide away on silk strands.

3 In the summer, spiderlings come out of the egg sac. There can be 800 spiderlings!

YOUR NEW WORDS

adult (**ah**-duhlt) a grown-up person or animal

arachnid (uh-**rak**-nid) an animal that has eight legs and two body parts

eggs (egs) oval or round objects in which baby birds, reptiles, and fish grow and change

moult (mohlt) to shed skin

sac (sak) a bag made of spider silk that holds spider eggs

silk (silk) thin strings that spiders make; spiderlings use them for gliding and making bridges

spiderling (**spy**-dur-ling) a baby spider

THESE ANIMALS HATCH FROM EGGS, TOO!

chicken

frog

shark

turtle

INDEX

FIND OUT MORE

Book:
Life Cycle of a Spider,
by Ron Fridell and Patricia Walsh (Heinemann Library, 2001)

Website:
http://www.enchantedlearning.com/subjects/arachnids/spider/

MEET THE AUTHOR:

Pam Zollman is a freelance writer of books, articles, and magazines for kids. She is the author of other books in the *Scholastic News Nonfiction Readers* series. She lives in rural Pennsylvania where she likes to watch spiders grow up in her backyard.